Trait-Based Writing Skills

Grades 2-3

by Connie S. Martin

Activities Support These Learning Outcomes:
- Students will add important details to their writing.
- Students will apply organizational skills to their writing.
- Students will use interesting and precise language.
- Students will incorporate techniques, such as dialogue and varied sentence structure, to create flow.
- Students will understand the importance of audience.
- Students will improve mechanics.
- Students will learn to assess writing.

Carson-Dellosa Publishing Company, Inc.
Greensboro, North Carolina

Credits

Editors
Ashley Futrell
Kelly Gunzenhauser

Layout Design
Jon Nawrocik

Inside Illustrations
George Ling

Cover Design
Peggy Jackson

© 2005, Carson-Dellosa Publishing Company, Inc., Greensboro, North Carolina 27425. The purchase of this material entitles the buyer to reproduce worksheets and activities for classroom use only—not for commercial resale. Reproduction of these materials for an entire school or district is prohibited. No part of this book may be reproduced (except as noted above), stored in a retrieval system, or transmitted in any form or by any means (mechanically, electronically, recording, etc.) without the prior written consent of Carson-Dellosa Publishing Co., Inc.

Printed in the USA • All rights reserved.   ISBN 1-59441-065-8

Table of Contents

INTRODUCTION............................ 3	SECTION 4: DOES MY WRITING FLOW?........... 22
SECTION 1: WHAT DO I WANT TO WRITE?......... 4	Varied Beginnings 24
Narrowing the Topic 6	Connectives 25
Managing Details 7	Dialogue 26
Collecting Details 8	Repeated Lines 27
Writing from Knowledge & Experience 9	SECTION 5: DOES MY WRITING SOUND LIKE ME? .. 28
SECTION 2: DOES MY WRITING HAVE GOOD	Talking on Paper 30
STRUCTURE?............................... 10	Writing for a Specific Audience 31
Tantalizing Titles 12	Narrative Writing 32
Who? What? When? Where? Why?.............. 13	Persuasive Writing............................ 33
Sequential Transitions 14	SECTION 6: IS MY WRITING CORRECT?.......... 34
Creative Conclusions 15	Editing for Spelling........................... 36
SECTION 3: HAVE I PAINTED A CLEAR PICTURE?... 16	Editing for Capitalization...................... 37
Vital Verbs.................................. 18	Editing for Punctuation....................... 38
Creative Color Words......................... 19	Editing for Grammar 39
Reviving Tired Language 20	ASSESSMENTS............................. 40
Painting a Mind Picture 21	Writing Rubric 41
	Section Assessments 43
	Answer Key .... inside back cover

Introduction

How many times have you carefully explained a writing assignment, only to look out at a sea of pitiful faces and blank stares? Some will wail mournfully, "I don't know what to write," while others will write about far too many topics at once. Students come to you with a variety of writing skills and varying levels of ability. How is it possible to accommodate each student? As a writing teacher, you can only accept students at their current levels and guide their growth.

The best way to serve as a writing guide is to model the thoughts and actions of a writer. In other words, teachers best teach writing by becoming writers. Show students how to think through the options for each aspect of a writing assignment, and they will feel more comfortable with the process and be empowered to become writers themselves.

If becoming a practicing, public writer for students sounds intimidating, remember that writing is simply telling something you want to share. Some students may be ready to share multipage stories. Others, especially second-language learners and very young children, may need to use a combination of drawing and writing to express an idea. Your goal is to teach writing skills while promoting an environment in which each child feels encouraged for all attempts at writing and respected when choosing to share that writing.

Trait-Based Writing Skills lessons provide grade-appropriate activities that require little planning or gathering of extra materials. Use them to teach and review trait-based writing skills, provide extra practice for individuals, or enhance any writing curriculum. Through these lessons, students will learn important trait-based language and methods and will also learn how to apply these skills to their own writing.

During the instruction portion of the lessons, model with the overhead projector or on chart paper to let students see your facial expressions as you verbalize thoughts and transfer those thoughts to writing. The reproducibles are sometimes incorporated within the teacher activities, but they are primarily designed for additional, independent practice of the lessons. Note that struggling writers at the second- and third-grade levels may need more modeling in order to understand and apply some concepts.

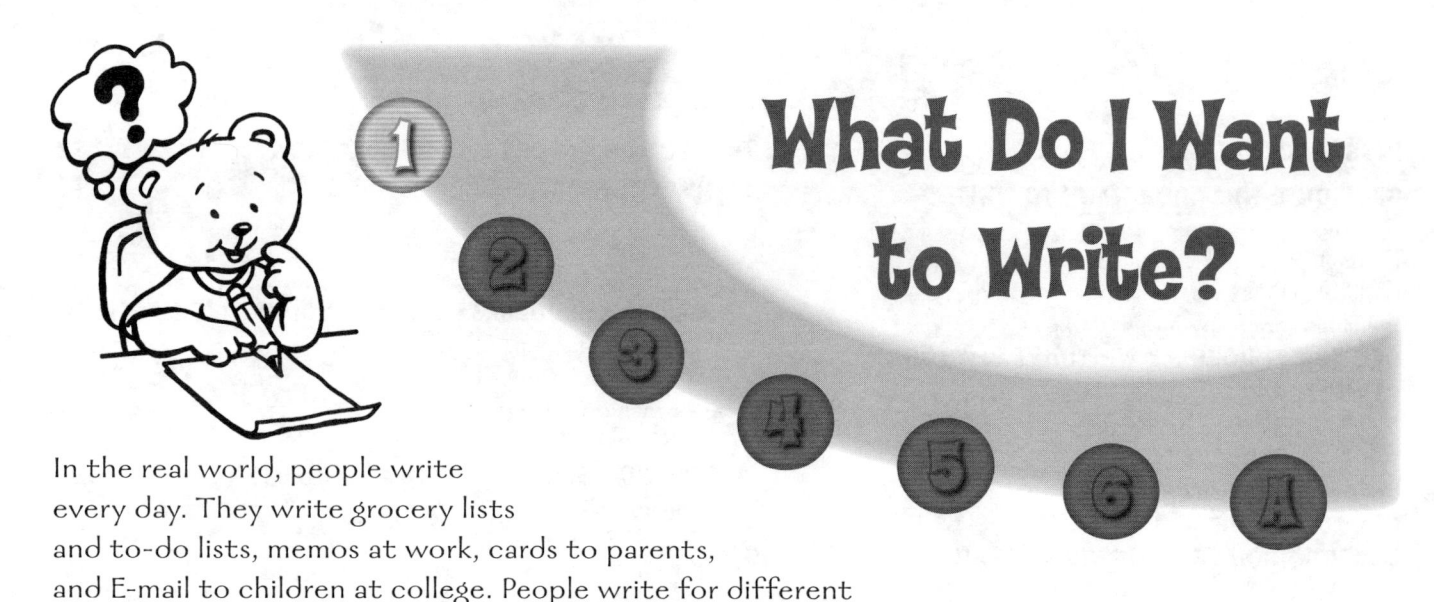

What Do I Want to Write?

In the real world, people write every day. They write grocery lists and to-do lists, memos at work, cards to parents, and E-mail to children at college. People write for different reasons, but they always write to effectively convey information. Students write for different reasons, too. Sometimes they simply write what they want to share, and sometimes they write for an assignment. They, too, need to write effectively. Effective writing begins when students are taught to consider a clear and organized topic and to include interesting supporting details. Writers are always more motivated and engaged in writing when they write about something that matters to them. Whenever possible, allow students to choose their own writing topics. The following activities will help students practice using the beginning skills they have already learned and fine-tune their skills in order to become effective writers.

Narrowing the Topic

Guide students to understand that a good topic is small enough to manage effectively. Tell them they should write about a topic you assign. On the board, write a topic they could not possibly manage, such as *Describe every day you have lived*, *Write about all of the animals in the world*, etc. Students will probably respond by complaining that they can't possibly do it. Ask why it is an impossible task, leading students to conclude that the topic must be something they know about or can research and must be easy to complete in a reasonable amount of time—which isn't very long for second and third graders. Show students a chart or transparency with a list of writing topics, some too large and some just right. Choose volunteers to circle the topics they think are too large and have them explain why. Have the class discuss each "oversized" topic and reach an agreement about the manageability. Brainstorm additional good choices for writing topics. Display the list for students to reference when choosing a writing topic. Some example topics to include:

- Instead of *Astronauts*, try *The First Man on the Moon*.
- Instead of *Weather*, try *What Makes a Tornado*.
- Instead of *Princesses*, try *The Story of Princess Virginia*.

Managing Details

Help students learn more about their classmates while organizing information. Give them copies of the *Detail Duty* worksheet (page 7). Create a transparency of the organizer. Tell students that the organizer will help them remember the important details they should include in their writing, no matter what the topic is. Choose a student to interview. Model how to complete the

What Do I Want to Write? ①

organizer with the topic (student's name) in the center and a word or phrase in each detail bubble as a reminder of what you want to share when you write. Pair students and have them brainstorm information they may want to learn about each other, such as favorite sports or games, dream jobs, wishes they would like to have granted, etc. Give students a few minutes to meet with their partners to ask questions and fill in their organizers. Have students write about the classmates they interviewed. Allow each student to share one new thing he learned. If time allows, share additional details or ask students why they chose to share their particular details.

Collecting Details

Tell students that you want to sell a bicycle and would like their opinion of an ad you have created to run in the newspaper. On the board or a transparency, show the following:

Bike for Sale.

Ask students for opinions about the ad. Some students will say they need to know more about the bike. Ask students what additional information should be included. They may mention color of bike, size, boy's or girl's, price, how to contact you, condition of bike, type of bike, etc. Tell students you really want to paint a picture in readers' minds so that they will know exactly what you are selling, and student suggestions for a complete description will help. Rewrite the ad, including the additional information, and have students decide which ad is best. Explain that you do not have a bike for sale, but you wanted them to see how important it is to include clear details. Give each student a page from colorful magazine ads or Sunday newspaper ads. Have each student circle the words in the ad that describe the item and tell why the words help paint a picture. Remind students to include descriptive details in their writing to paint complete pictures in readers' minds.

Writing from Knowledge & Experience

On a transparency or a piece of chart paper, create two versions of a paragraph using a topic students currently are studying or the following examples. Read and discuss each version with students. Ask which version tells more about the topic and paints a clearer picture in readers' minds. Choose students to underline sentences that give clear information about the topic. Guide students to state that writing—fiction or nonfiction—is more effective and interesting if specific information—rather than vague statements—is included.

Version 1: Pet Snakes

There are lots of snakes in the United States. Snakes are slithery. I think snakes would be very good pets unless they are the kind that bite.

Version 2: Snakes

Snakes are interesting creatures. Some snakes make good pets. One of the most popular pet snakes is the corn snake. It is also known as the red rat snake. The corn snake is a good choice for a pet because it is not poisonous, is easy to take care of, eats a wide variety of foods, and usually does not bite unless it is scared.

What Do I Want to Write? ①   NARROWING THE TOPIC

NAME _____

TOPIC TRAINING

Directions: Read the topics in each line. Circle the topic in each line that would be just right to manage. Then, answer the question and follow the directions at the bottom of the page.

1. Plants   Cactus   Desert plants

2. My life   Birthdays   My best birthday

3. Planets   Mars   Solar system

4. Board games   Games   How to play checkers

5. My brother Mike   Brothers and sisters   Families

1. Why would it be hard to write about the topics you did not circle?

_____

2. On the lines below, write a list of five topics that would be too big. Then, write a list of five topics that would be easy to write about.

_____   _____

_____   _____

_____   _____

_____   _____

_____   _____

What Do I Want to Write? ①

MANAGING DETAILS

NAME _____

DETAIL DUTY

Directions: List your writing topic in the center circle. In the other circles, write a word or words to remind you of a detail you want to share about the topic.

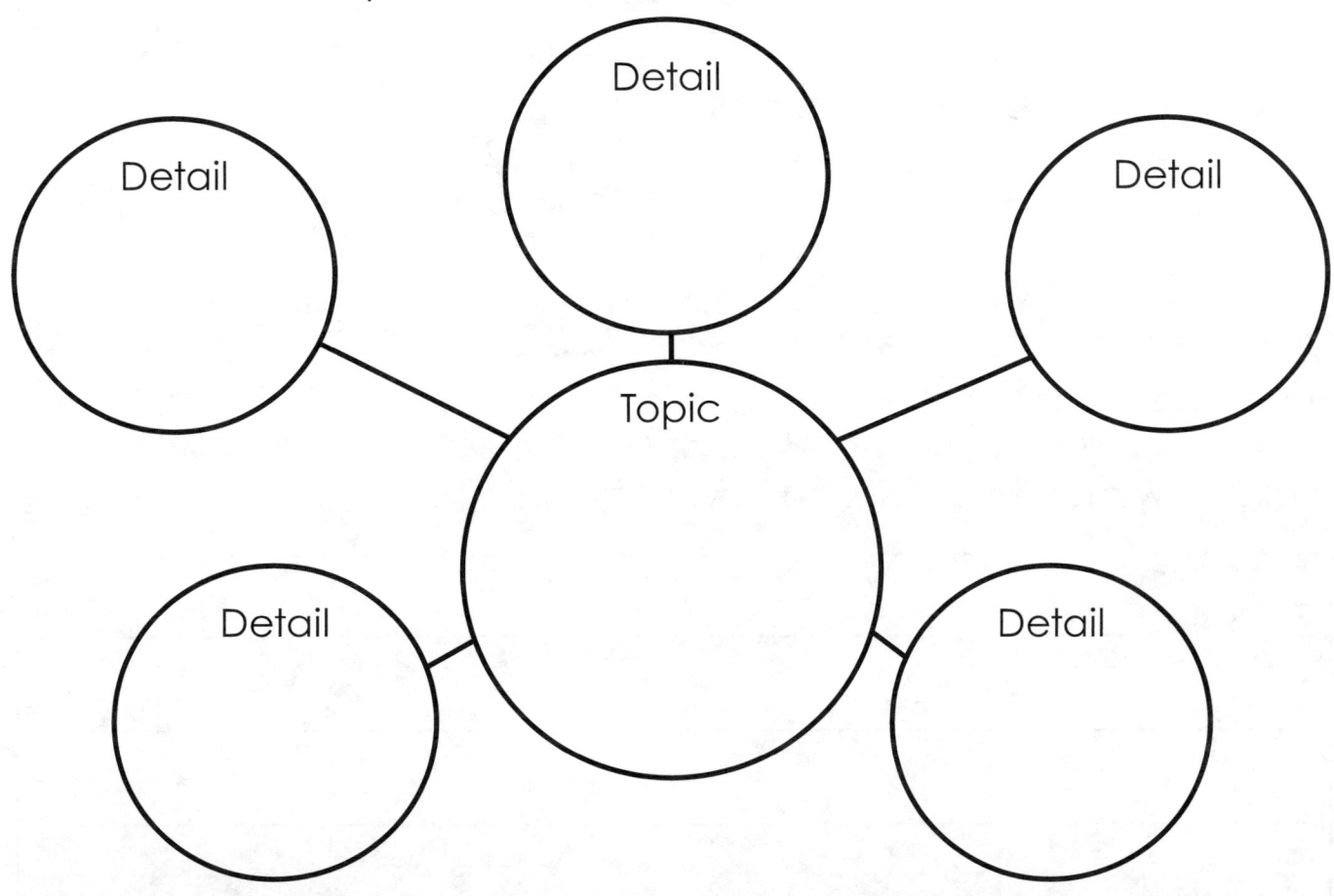

- Detail
- Detail
- Detail
- Topic
- Detail
- Detail

EXTRA

On a separate piece of paper, answer the following questions:
Are these the best details to include? Why or why not?
Did you leave out any important details?
Are these good, specific details, or can you be more specific?
Now, explain why this is a good topic.

What Do I Want to Write? ①   **COLLECTING DETAILS**

NAME _____

DETAIL DETECTIVE

Directions: Read the ad. Circle each word that helps tell more about the items for sale.

Toy Sale
- black-and-white striped skateboard $8.00
- small, blonde-haired doll with blue dress, white shoes, and polka-dot hat $2.00
- set of 24 football trading cards $1.00

Call 321-555-1234

Think about a toy you would like to pretend to sell. Write an ad to sell your toy. Be sure to tell important details like what the toy is, how it looks, how much it costs, and how to contact you.

For Sale: _____

_____

_____

_____

_____

Now, circle the words in your ad that tell details about the toy. Answer the following questions on a separate piece of paper.

1. Why are these words important?
2. How will these words help you sell the toy better?

What Do I Want to Write? ① WRITING FROM KNOWLEDGE & EXPERIENCE

NAME _____

FAMILY TIME

Directions: Read the two paragraphs. Then, answer the questions and follow the directions at the bottom of the page.

Ann's Family

I have a big family. They are nice. My family does lots of things with me. We play together and sometimes we work together. Sometimes we go on trips. My family loves me very much.

Robert's Family

I have a big family. I have two brothers and three sisters. Tom is 18, and Samuel is 16. I am 8. My sister Kathleen is 14, Sara is 12, and Susan is 4. My family and I usually get along pretty well. When we do argue, Mom makes us sit down and talk about the problem until we work it out. My brothers and I like to play football together. I'm not so great, but Tom is helping me learn to throw the ball better. Every Saturday my family cleans the house together. I help Mom by dusting. It's not much fun, but if we all work together we get it done fast! Then, we get to do something fun, like going to race bumper cars. I love that! I know my family loves me because we work and play together, and we really care about each other, even if we do argue sometimes.

1. Whose paragraph tells more about the topic? _____

2. Why is this a better paragraph? _____

_____

3. On a separate piece of paper, write three things you learned about Ann's family and three things you learned about Robert's family. Use complete sentences in your answers.

Does My Writing Have Good Structure?

Just as a fine recipe begins with the selection of quality ingredients and a strong building stands on a firm foundation, good writing must begin with a sound structure. Good writing is based on a focused topic that is introduced in an engaging manner with details organized logically to transition smoothly from point to point. The writing provides answers to readers' *who, what, when, where,* and *how* questions and leaves them feeling satisfied, yet wishing there were more. Whether the writing consists of three paragraphs or three pages, the characteristics of good writing remain the same.

Tantalizing Titles

Display a variety of books. Choose some with dull titles, as well as some with titles that invite the reader in, such as *A Treeful of Pigs* by Arnold Lobel (William, Morrow & Co., 1987), *More Spaghetti, I Say* by Rita Golden Gelman (Scholastic, 1998), *The Adventures of Taxi Dog* by Debra and Sal Barracca (Puffin, 2000), *Feathers for Lunch* by Lois Ehlert (Harcourt, 1990), and *Lilly's Purple Plastic Purse* by Kevin Henkes (William, Morrow & Co., 1996). (Some emergent reader titles are only one word, so these might work well for the dull titles.) Share the titles with students and ask them to guess what each book might be about after looking only at the covers and titles. Have students determine which titles are most inviting and why. Place the books in the reading center for students to explore. Now, assign students to small groups. Give each group a copy of the paragraph below or one you create. Have students in each group read and discuss the paragraph and choose an interesting title. Let each group share their title and explain why they chose it. Students will find there can be several interesting and appropriate titles for the same piece of writing.

Example:

    Boy, was I scared! We should have known better than to go into that old cave at sunset. Overgrown weeds and spiderwebs covered the opening, but we pushed our way through until we were standing in the dark inside the cave. It was so dark, we couldn't even see each other! We didn't go far before we heard the awful sound—like a monster with a thousand wings was coming our way. We took off for the opening and practically jumped over each other to be the first one out. Then, we ran for the bushes because the noise behind us was getting louder and louder. Finally, we saw hundreds of bats fly out of the cave, flapping their wings and diving at us! That was close, but we were safe in the bushes. I'll never go back to that cave. It definitely belongs to the bats!

Does My Writing Have Good Structure? ②

Who? What? When? Where? Why?

Plan this lesson for individuals, pairs of students, or small groups. Distribute pictures from catalogs, magazines, newspapers, or collections of famous paintings. Ask each student to study her picture and decide *who* she thinks is in it, *what* is happening, *when* it is happening, *where* it is taking place, and *why* the event is occurring. Each student may imagine something silly or serious, as long as she can justify her reasoning using the images in her picture. Choose students to share their pictures and imaginings. Ask the class to suggest other possibilities for the pictures shared. Guide students to state that the more specific the given information is, the easier it will be to understand. Explain that students should also give specific information in their writing in order for others to understand their meaning. Close the activity by having each student write a descriptive paragraph about her picture. Collect the paragraphs, comment on good uses of description that answer all of the questions, and return the papers.

Sequential Transitions

Share the paragraph below, or create a similar paragraph based on a topic students are studying. Read in a monotone voice, emphasizing the continued repetition of the words *and then*. Ask students to comment on how the paragraph sounds. Someone will probably acknowledge the repetitious use of certain words and the run-on sentences. Ask students for suggestions for improving the paragraph. Brainstorm a list of sequential transition words (*first, next, then, also, afterward, at last, finally,* etc.). Create a transparency of the paragraph with blanks inserted for transitions. Have students suggest transition words to fill in the blanks. Read the paragraph again with the transition words in place. Students should notice that the paragraph is easier to follow and is more interesting when the transition words are used.

Example: How to Make a Banana Split
Put three scoops of ice cream in a dish and then peel a banana and then slice it down the middle and then put half of the banana on each side of the ice cream. And then add chocolate syrup on top and then put whipped cream on top of the syrup. And then sprinkle nuts on top of everything and then add a cherry on top. And then eat your banana split!

Creative Conclusions

Read aloud a short story that students have never heard, but stop before the ending is revealed. Have students suggest possible endings or have them write endings for the story and share them with the class. Discuss which new endings seem most interesting and why. Make a list of the characteristics of a creative ending, including such items as: *It answers questions posed in the story, It has a surprise ending, It makes the reader wish there were more, It makes a person really think about how the story relates to real life,* etc. Display the list for students to reference when writing. Read the story's real ending. Have students decide which ending seems to be the most satisfying and why. All students may not agree. To extend the activity, assign students to groups and let each group act out the story using a different ending.

Does My Writing Have Good Structure? ② TANTALIZING TITLES

NAME _____

HOME RUN HEADLINES

Directions: Read the paragraph. Choose the best title from the list and write it in the blank at the top of the paragraph. Then, answer the questions.

A Ball Game   A Sad Day   The Season Finale

_____

   It was the last game of the season. We were losing 8 to 6 in the last inning. I just knew we had a chance of winning if Luis could hit a home run. The first pitch whizzed by . . . strike one. The next pitch was a foul ball. Then, pitch number three sailed right above home plate! Luis smacked the ball, and it went sailing into right field! Luis was on his way to second base when their player ran back and caught the ball right in his mitt. The season was over. We lost. I was so disappointed, but we had a great season, and we always had fun. Just wait until next year!

1. Why do you think your choice is the best title? _____

_____

2. Can you think of better titles for the story? Write at least 3 suggestions.

_____

_____

EXTRA

On a separate piece of paper, write five crazy, silly, funny, or scary titles. Be sure to make them interesting. Pick one and write a short story. Or, trade papers with a friend and use one of your friend's titles to help you write a story.

Does My Writing Have Good Structure? ② WHO? WHAT? WHEN? WHERE? WHY?

NAME _____

A SPECIAL DAY

Directions: Read the paragraph. Then, answer the questions.

   Last summer, Maria and Lucy won free tickets to the water park. At the park, they floated down the lazy river ride and jumped the waves in the wave pool. They even slid down the tallest water slide in the park! The girls ate frosty snow cones and cheesy pizza. By the end of the day, they were wet and tired, but happy. It had been a great day at the water park!

1. Who is in the story? _____

2. Where did they go? _____

3. What four things did they do there? _____
_____
_____

4. When did they go? _____

5. Why did they get to go there? _____

EXTRA
On a separate piece of paper, write about a time when you went to a special place. Tell *who*, *what*, *when*, *where*, and *why*. Then, trade papers with a classmate. Find answers to the *who*, *what*, *when*, *where*, and *why* questions. Circle them on your classmate's paper.

Does My Writing Have Good Structure? ② | SEQUENTIAL TRANSITIONS

NAME _____

HOW TO WASH A DOG

Directions: *Sequential* means *in order*. Use words from the Word Box to fill in the blanks to show a logical order of events when washing a dog. Remember to put commas after transition words. There may be more than one correct word for a blank. Use each word only once.

Word Box
First Also At last
Next Afterward Then
Finally

_____ fill a big wash tub with warm water. _____ put the dog in the wash tub. _____ wash the dog with soapy dog shampoo. _____ rinse him with warm water. _____ get a big, fluffy towel. _____ dry him off. _____ let your dog shake and shake until he is dry!

Think about something you like to do. Write the directions, using words from the Word Box to help explain the correct order.

_____

_____

_____

_____

Does My Writing Have Good Structure? 2   CREATIVE CONCLUSIONS

NAME _____

LOST!

Directions: Read the story. Then, write two different endings for the story.

    We were lost in the mountains with no one around. We must have taken a wrong turn on the trail. The sun was going down, and it was beginning to get cold. We didn't have anything to eat or drink because I had slipped and dropped my backpack over the side of the hill. We decided to keep walking, hoping we would meet other hikers who could show us the way out. We walked for a while in the dark until we saw a light shining on the trail ahead of us. We started to run to the light, but just then . . .

1. Write a happy ending for the story.

_____
_____
_____
_____

2. Write the second ending any way you like, but make it different from the first one you wrote.

_____
_____
_____
_____

Have I Painted a Clear Picture?

A writer's goal is to clearly convey the information he wants to share by choosing specific words and phrases that create clear pictures in readers' minds. Students can learn to review the words in their writing, consider the pictures they want to paint in readers' minds, and replace old, tired, overused words and phrases with rich, vibrant vocabulary. Help students learn that they should create just the right pictures so that readers can understand what is being shared. Then, expose students to the skills they need to paint those pictures in readers' minds.

Vital Verbs

Prepare a simple sentence to place in a pocket chart (example: *I went around the track.*). Create a series of word cards with vibrant, alternate verbs that show specific action. Make some silly and make some serious (example verbs: *raced, zoomed, flew, danced, sped, dashed*). Place the cards in a box or bag. Choose a student to select a card, read the verb, and place the word card in the pocket chart under the verb *went*. Explain that each new word will make students think of a different action. Let the volunteer student act out the new sentence or choose another student who would like to act it out. Or, have a student act out the new verb and have others guess the verb before displaying the word card in the pocket chart. Repeat the procedure with a new simple sentence, such as: *I said, "Stop, thief!"* (possible verb cards: *shouted, screamed, yelled, whispered, whimpered*). Finally, ask students to choose the most interesting verbs and explain their choices.

Creative Color Words

Before the lesson, collect free paint-color sample squares from a local home improvement store. The names for many paint colors are vivid descriptions for basic colors, such as blueberry, sapphire, shamrock, strawberry, etc. Read aloud a book about colors, such as *The Colors of Us* by Karen Katz (Henry Holt and Company, 1999). This book describes the skin colors of a young girl and her friends, using wonderfully descriptive words and phrases for *brown*. Read the story again, asking students to raise a hand each time another word for *brown* is used. Have students identify the descriptive words. Tell students there are better ways to describe other colors, as well. Assign students to six groups: red, blue, green, orange, yellow, and purple. Give each group a piece of poster board or chart paper and a selection of paint-color samples for their color family. Have students read the name on each paint sample and discuss why it is a more descriptive word for the color. Have them think about the mind picture each name creates. Have each group write the basic color word in the center of their chart, glue the samples around the word, and label each sample to easily identify it

Have I Painted a Clear Picture? ③

from a distance. Let students brainstorm more descriptive color words to add to their charts. Have each group share their information. Display the charts for students to reference when writing.

Reviving Tired Language

On a set of index cards, write a variety of overused words, such as *pretty, nice, happy, good, bad, fine, love,* etc. For each overused word, write three synonyms on individual cards. For example, for the word *pretty,* write *attractive, beautiful,* and *lovely.* Keep the cards for overused words and distribute the synonym cards. Draw an overused word card and place it in a pocket chart. Discuss the meaning with students. Ask students to hold up their cards if they think their words mean about the same as the word in the pocket chart. Discuss each word card and place the synonyms in a row next to the overused word. Repeat with each overused word. Tell students they can choose a variety of words when writing instead of using the same tired words. Next, explain that a thesaurus is a book filled with synonyms and antonyms. Have each student create a personal thesaurus. Give students sheets of lined paper to staple together to make blank books. Have them label the pages alphabetically and then write overused words on the appropriate pages. Next, have each student list three synonyms beside each word. Let students keep these thesauruses in their writing folders for reference. Continue adding new words to the thesauruses throughout the year.

Painting a Mind Picture

Share a story about different kinds of houses or share the following poem with students.

> Would you like to live in a house in a tree?
> Or perhaps in a houseboat that sails on the sea?
> You might live in the forest in your very own tent,
> Or in a big city in a fine apartment.
> Maybe you'd live in a house on a street,
> Where children are playing and the yard's always neat.
> Just dream of the place you might live in one day—
> Your own special place where you'll sleep and you'll play.

Have students close their eyes and think about where they now live or imagine where they would like to live. Ask students to create pictures in their minds as you ask questions to help them form the images. For example, ask, "Where is your home, in the city or the country? Is it made of brick, wood, or siding? What color is it? Are there windows? Is there a chimney? Is there a yard or a play area? Are there trees, bushes, or flowers out front? Are there toys in the yard? What kind? Is there a big porch, a small porch, or no porch? If there is a porch, is anything on it? What is around your home: other houses or buildings, the forest, the ocean, city buildings, a park?" Have students draw pictures of the homes in their minds and write descriptions. Tell them to include the answers to your questions in their descriptions. Explain that the more details they include, the clearer the pictures will be in readers' minds.

Have I Painted a Clear Picture? 3

VITAL VERBS

NAME _____

READY, SET, GO!

Directions: Read the sentences. Rewrite each sentence, replacing the underlined verb with a stronger verb from the word box.

Word Box

| splashed | smacked | sprinted | soared |
| yelled | tumbled | yanked | |

1. "Go team, go!" **said** the cheerleaders.

2. Josh **pulled** the cord to start the lawn mower.

3. The jet **went** up into the sky.

4. Sarah **ran** across the finish line to win the race.

5. We **walked** through the rain puddles on the way to school.

6. The birthday presents **fell** when I opened the door.

7. Thomas **hit** the ball for a home run.

Have I Painted a Clear Picture? 3

CREATIVE COLOR WORDS

NAME _____

TREASURE HUNT

Directions: Read each color word and the list of synonyms. Then, read the paragraph. Choose descriptive synonyms to fill in the blank before each color word in order to paint a picture in readers' minds. Use the color words below to help you, or think of your own words that are not on the list. You may want to look in the dictionary to understand words that are new to you.

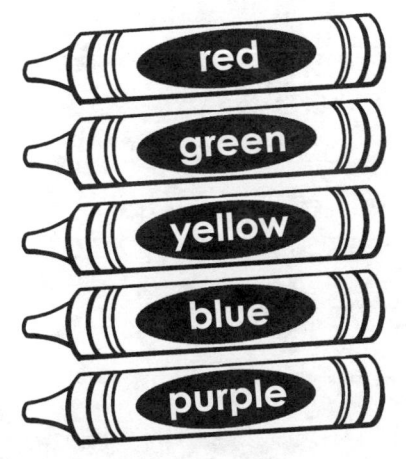

- red — ruby, crimson, scarlet, cherry
- green — jade, sage, emerald, lime
- yellow — gold, lemon, amber, saffron
- blue — sapphire, navy, aqua, turquoise
- purple — plum, violet, grape, lavender

The knight paused before entering the forest. He was on a journey to find treasure! He hoped to find a _____ (red) ring and a necklace of _____ (blue). The _____ (yellow) sun shone brightly in the sky. The knight gazed at the beautiful _____ (green) trees swaying slightly in the breeze and at a bunch of _____ (purple) flowers growing near the edge of the path. He took a deep breath and plunged into the forest.

EXTRA

On a separate piece of paper, use color words to describe what you would find if you discovered a treasure chest.

Have I Painted a Clear Picture? ③   **REVIVING TIRED LANGUAGE**

NAME _____

SIZZLING SYNONYMS

Directions: Read each sentence. Use the Word Box to choose a synonym for the bold word. Fill in each blank to create a more descriptive sentence. Not all words will be used.

Word Box

scorching	sizzling	sweltering	chilly	icy
frosty	pleasant	kind	agreeable	sob
weep	angry	upset	furious	snip
trim	amusing	comical	witty	enjoyable
excellent	satisfying	adore	cherish	appreciate

1. **hot:** It was a _____ day in the desert.

2. **cold:** It was so _____ we had to put on hats and gloves before we could go out.

3. **cry:** The little boy began to _____ because he could not find his cat.

4. **cut:** Please help me _____ the dog's fur.

5. **funny:** We thought the circus clown was very _____ .

6. **mad:** Dad was really _____ when we broke the window.

7. **good:** Mom makes a/an _____ dinner every Friday night!

8. **like:** I _____ my sister, even if she is sometimes a pain.

Have I Painted a Clear Picture? ③ — PAINTING A MIND PICTURE

NAME _____

MY DREAM ROOM

Directions: You will need a separate piece of paper for this activity. Think about your dream bedroom. Imagine yourself standing in the doorway and think about everything you see. Look around the room and write about what you see. First, write the answers to the questions. Then, write a paragraph about the room. Give details to paint a clear picture in readers' minds.

1. What color is the paint or wallpaper?
2. Are there curtains, shades, or shutters? How do they look?
3. Tell about the rug or floor.
4. Describe the furniture. What color is it? What kinds of furniture do you have—bed, desk, chair, sofa, chest?
5. Are there pictures or posters on the wall? Describe them.
6. What is on the shelves?
7. Are there toys and games? Tell about them.
8. Do you have your own room, or do you share with someone?
9. Is your room clean or messy? Who keeps it that way?
10. How does the room smell?
11. Share anything else about your room that you want to tell.

EXTRA

On a separate piece of paper, draw a picture of your dream bedroom. When you are finished, look back at the writing. Does your picture match the description you wrote?

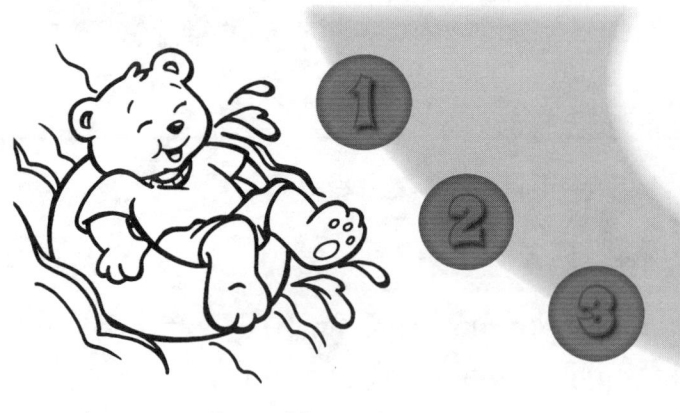

Does My Writing Flow?

Good writing flows like a river. Sentences that begin in a variety of ways, sentences of differing lengths, the addition of dialogue when appropriate, and techniques, such as repeating lines (or using fragments on purpose), offer the writer tools to sculpt the writing like time sculpts a riverbed. The river may be serene in some places and ferocious in others. Writing may sometimes make us mellow and sometimes cause us to feel intense emotion. Good writing is always easy to read and understand. Readers are caught in the "current" of the writing and follow it to the conclusion. Readers take a pleasant trip down the river, and the writing flows.

Varied Beginnings

Rewrite a paragraph from a science or social studies text that students are studying so that each sentence begins the same way, or use the following example. Make a copy for each student. Read the paragraph to students, accentuating the word or phrase that begins each sentence. Have students highlight the first word or phrase in each sentence. Ask what they notice. Ask students how the words in the sentences can be rearranged so that all of the sentences do not begin in the same way. Rewrite the paragraph on a piece of chart paper or a transparency, making the changes suggested by students. Model the first change for them. Read both versions and have students decide which is more interesting and easier to follow.

Example:
We went to the mall last Saturday. We played with puppies and lizards at the pet store. We listened to new CDs at the music store. We tried on cool sunglasses and hats at the department store. We ate pizza for lunch. We had a great time at the mall even though we didn't spend a lot of money. We know our parents were happy about that!

Connectives

We can use the words *and*, *or*, and *but* to show connections between things and depict logical order. On separate sentence strips, prepare several pairs of clauses that can be connected using one of these words. For example, write *I like chocolate ice cream. I do not like vanilla.* The connective would be *but*. Give each student three index cards. Have students write *and* on one card, *but* on one card, and *or* on one card. Choose two students to come to the front and display two paired clauses. Have the rest of the class hold up the word cards that they think would correctly connect the clauses to make a compound sentence. Read the new sentence using each

Does My Writing Flow? ④

connective and have students decide which fits. In some cases, more than one connective will fit. Repeat with all of the prepared clauses. Other clause pairs to consider are:

- You may have pancakes. You may have waffles.
- Birds build nests. Birds lay eggs.
- Tomás went to the baseball game. His brother Ramón caught a foul ball.
- Iris loves to sing. Iris does not like to dance.
- Joey may want to read books. Joey may want to play a game.

Dialogue

Provide a selection of comic strips. Have students read and share a few of them. Ask students how they know what is being said and who is speaking each time. Someone will probably suggest that the speech balloons contain what is being said and are pointed toward the speakers. Choose a piece of writing containing dialogue, such as a page from a current basal or trade book. Or, you may wish to obtain copies of one of Aesop's fables. (These fables are useful because they are short and easy to access.) Choose a selection that is appropriate for students' reading levels. Read the selection with students. Ask how they know what is being said and who is speaking since there are no speech balloons. Explain the use of quotation marks to identify the words being spoken. Have students draw circles around each set of quotation marks along with the words between them. Then, have them underline the name of the character who is speaking each time. Discuss who is speaking and what is being said, and explain that dialogue can add to the interest of a piece of writing. Encourage students to include dialogue in their writing.

Repeated Lines

Make sure students understand that using repeated text is a technique writers can use to create a poetic effect. It is very different from using the same sentence beginning over and over without a purpose. Choose books that contain one or more repeated lines of text to share with students. Some good examples are: *Wombat Stew* by Marcia Vaughn (Silver Burdett Press, 1986), *A Giraffe and a Half* by Shel Silverstein (Harper Collins, 1964), *The Book That Jack Wrote* by Jon Scieszka (Viking, 1994), *Meanwhile, Back at the Ranch* by Trina Hakes Nobel (Puffin Books, 1992), *That's Good! That's Bad! in the Grand Canyon* by Margery Cuyler (Henry Holt and Company, 2002), *When I Was Young in the Mountains* by Cynthia Rylant (E. P. Dutton, 1982).

Read and discuss one story with students and ask if they noticed that part of the text repeats. Read the story again and have students raise their hands each time they hear the repeated text. Have them decide if the repetition adds to the enjoyment of the story. Why or why not? If there is time for a third reading, let students act out the story as you read it. Choose individual student actors for the main part of the text. Then, have the rest of the class join the chorus, calling out the repeated text each time. Repeat this with other selections to emphasize the concept of repeated text. Finally, ask each student to write a short paragraph explaining when it is and is not acceptable to begin sentences with the same word or phrase. Collect and evaluate the paragraphs.

Does My Writing Flow?

VARIED BEGINNINGS

NAME _____

BALLPARK BEGINNINGS

Directions: Read the paragraph. Underline the first word in each sentence. Rewrite the paragraph and change the beginnings of the sentences so that they are not all the same. To do this, you can change the order of the words, use synonyms for some words, add transition words, or combine sentences.

   I had such fun at the baseball game! I threw speed pitch with my friends. I ate a hot dog for dinner. I ate chips, too. I had ice cream in a plastic bowl that was shaped like a baseball cap. I almost caught a foul ball! I watched fireworks after dark. I can't wait to go to another exciting baseball game.

CONJUNCTION FUNCTION

Directions: Complete each sentence by filling in the blank with the word *and*, *but*, or *or*.

1. I like to eat hamburgers _____ french fries for dinner.

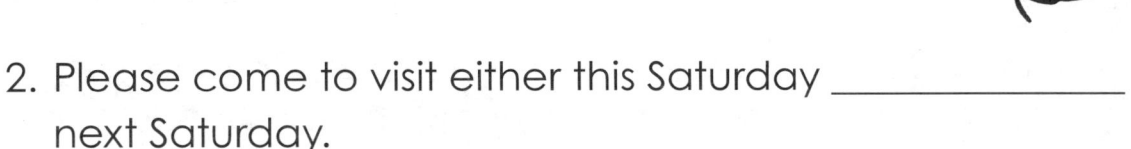

2. Please come to visit either this Saturday _____ next Saturday.

3. I don't like to get shots, _____ I do like to get a prize at the doctor's office.

4. May we please go both to dinner _____ to a movie?

5. I want a new bike, _____ I can't buy it until I earn enough money.

6. Mom said I may have a cat _____ a dog but not both.

7. May I have a bacon, lettuce, _____ tomato sandwich?

8. I will have to decide if I want roller blades _____ a skateboard for my birthday, but I cannot have both.

EXTRA
On a separate piece of paper, write three sentences about yourself. Use a different connecting word in each sentence.

Does My Writing Flow? — DIALOGUE

MOVIE MADNESS

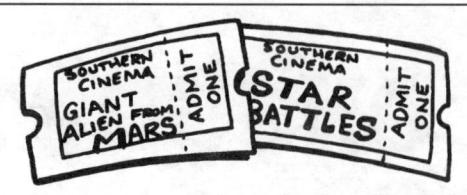

NAME _____

Directions: Read the story. Draw a circle around all of the quotation marks (" ") and the words between them that show what is being said. Underline the words that tell who is talking each time. The first one has been done for you. Then, answer the questions on a separate piece of paper.

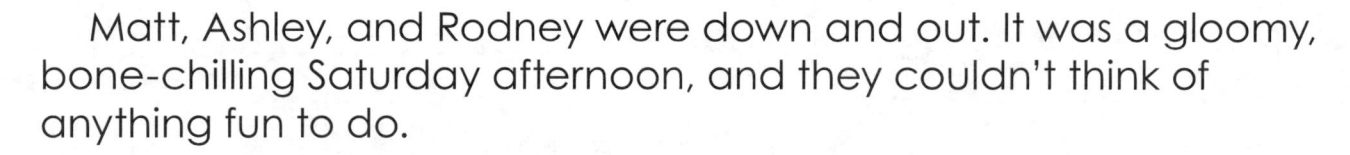

Matt, Ashley, and Rodney were down and out. It was a gloomy, bone-chilling Saturday afternoon, and they couldn't think of anything fun to do.

("Let's go to a movie,") <u>suggested Ashley</u>.

"That's a great idea! Which movie should we see?" Matt asked.

"I don't care as long as it has lots of action and adventure,"

Rodney said.

Ashley said, "I think we should see *The Treasure of Mystery Mountain*."

"Good idea," said Matt. "I heard that one is a winner!"

"Let's go," said Rodney. "Popcorn, here we come!"

1. Do you think they will have a good time at the movie? Write a conversation that you think the friends might have after the movie.

2. Why do you think dialogue is important in a piece of writing?

Does My Writing Flow?

REPEATED LINES

NAME _____

DON'T BE LATE!

Directions: Underline the repeated sentence in the story each time it appears. On a separate piece of paper, write about what you think happened next in the story. Use the repeated sentence in your writing.

Wilfred Wondergast was running to school. He was in a terrible hurry because he didn't listen when his mom said, "Get up!" Now, he was late. Wilfred kept running. Right around the corner hopped a giant, five-legged, three-eyed, purple-polka-dotted frog! It jumped right over Wilfred and hopped down the street. Wilfred kept running. Just around the next corner came a huge Tyrannosaurus Rex. It sneered at Wilfred and ran down the street. Wilfred kept running. He was trying to get to school, when just around the next corner . . .

Why do you think the author used the same sentence over and over?

_____

_____

EXTRA

On a separate piece of paper, write several short sentences. Choose one sentence and write a story that uses it several times. What effect are you trying to create by using this sentence?

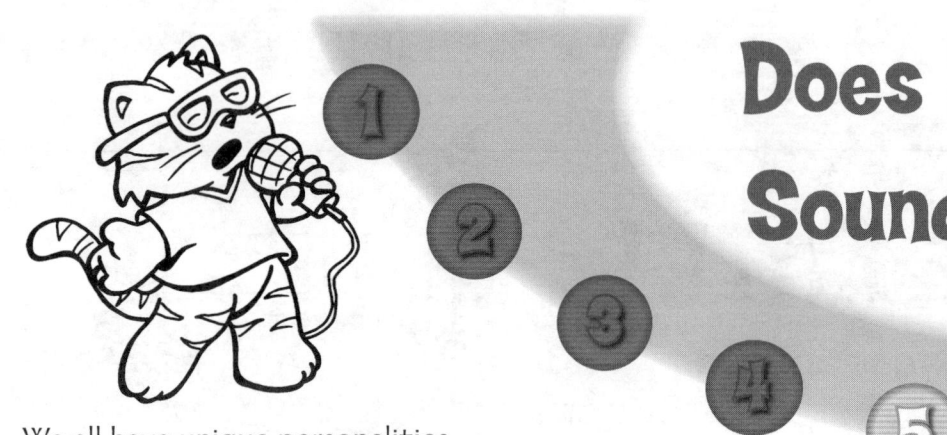

Does My Writing Sound Like Me?

We all have unique personalities. We view the world from our own perspectives and express ourselves as individuals. Writing gives us a vehicle for individual expression. We immediately see a difference in the writing of *Alice in Wonderland* by Lewis Carroll (W.W. Norton & Company; 2nd edition, 1989) and *The Cat in the Hat* by Dr. Seuss (Random House Books for Young Readers, 1957). Each author lets his own personality and perspective shine. The writer strives to share authentic thoughts and feelings—almost as though he is holding a conversation with readers and "talking on paper." The tone of a piece of writing depends on the specific audience and purpose for writing. Readers, in turn, should feel a strong connection with the writer and believe in the writer's commitment to the work.

The best way to help students begin to understand this concept is to read aloud several pieces of literature that highlight the unique sound and personality of each author. Then, have students try to make their own writing sound unique. Some excellent books to share are:

- *The Year of the Perfect Christmas Tree* by Gloria Houston (Dial Books for Young Readers, 1988)
- *Alexander and the Terrible, Horrible, No Good, Very Bad Day* by Judith Viorst (Aladdin, 1987)
- *Nate the Great and Me: The Case of the Fleeing Fang* by Marjorie Weinman Sharmat (Delacorte Press, 1998)
- *Sweet Clara and the Freedom Quilt* by Deborah Hopkinson (Alfred A. Knopf, Inc., 1993)
- *Voices in the Park* by Anthony Browne (DK Publishing, Inc., 1998)
- Poetry by Jack Prelutsky or Shel Silverstein

Talking on Paper

Choose several books from the list above or select other books that have a distinctive voice. Read aloud passages from the books. Ask students if the characters sound like real people talking to friends and sharing their thoughts. Why or why not? Discuss the type of vocabulary that is used. Would the characters use those words? If slang or fragments are used, is it appropriate for the time and place? What can you tell about a character's personality just by hearing what he has to say within a small part of the story? How are the characters different? Are they the same in any way? Which books would be the most fun to read? Discuss how each author shows a unique personality in her writing. Keep the books in a reading center for students to read and enjoy.

Does My Writing Sound Like Me? ⑤

Writing for a Specific Audience

Collect or create a variety of writing samples to share with students, such as brief newspaper and magazine articles, letters, memos, reminder notes, grocery lists, phone messages, E-mails, recipes, invitations, research notes, outlines, and reports. Distribute the samples for students to review. Have volunteers read several of the writing samples. Ask what they have in common. Help students realize that each one is a form of writing and its purpose is to communicate some type of information. Discuss the differences in the writing samples and decide the audience for each. Have students decide if the formality of the writing depends on the audience. For example, a grocery list or reminder note written for yourself may contain words or phrases rather than complete sentences with correct punctuation. A friendly letter is more casual than a report. Have students brainstorm other types of writing. After you write several types on the board, ask students to name a possible audience for each type. Write the audiences on the board, as well. Remind students to consider the audience and purpose when they write.

Narrative Writing

Share a book or story that details a day or an event in an animal's life from the animal's first person perspective. A few good choices are: *I Am the Dog, I Am the Cat* by Donald Hall (Dial Books, 1994), *The Windhover* by Alan Brown (Harcourt, Brace, and Co., 1997), and *And to Think That I Saw It on Mulberry Street* by Dr. Seuss (Random House Books for Young Readers; Reissue edition, 1989). Explain that in narrative writing the author tells a story from a character's point of view. For each book, ask if students think the author did a good job of showing what it would be like to be that character. Let them choose specific passages that show how the character would think and feel.

Persuasive Writing

Have students consider a current issue in your class, school, or town, such as the necessity of homework, the amount of homework assigned each night, the clothes students should or shouldn't be allowed to wear to school, or whether soda should be available in the lunch room. Choose an issue that will get strong reactions. Have each student cast an initial vote to find out the majority opinion on the topic. Then, let students debate the issue, citing reasons for their opinions. After the debate, have students reconsider their positions. Let students use the *I Think I'm Right* worksheet (page 33) to organize their thoughts and to write about their final opinions, including reasons for their decisions. Make sure students identify the audience for their writing. Let volunteers share their writing and then take a final class vote on the issue. If possible, share the information with those responsible for making the decision.

> **Putting an Exclamation Point on It**
>
> *This exercise is also useful when teaching students about debates and persuasive speaking during social studies units on the election process.*

Does My Writing Sound Like Me? ⑤ — TALKING ON PAPER

NAME _____

"OH, WOE IS ME!"

Directions: Read the journal entry of a boy who has moved to a new town. Think about how he feels and the words he uses to "talk on paper." Then, answer the questions on a separate piece of paper.

August 12

    I can't believe my parents have made me move to this terrible town. It's so unfair! Nobody asked me if I wanted to move. I don't see why my dad couldn't just find another job in our old town. Sometimes I really think they just do stuff like this to make me miserable! Now, I have to go to a new school where I don't know anybody. Maybe I'll just pretend to be sick tomorrow so I won't have to go, but then I'll just have to go the next day. Wait! From my bedroom window I can see a girl coming down the street. She looks nice, but I bet she's not. Hey! She's stopping in front of my house. She's coming up the walk. I hear the doorbell. Maybe she's going to ask me to come to her house. Maybe she's nice. Maybe she'll be my new best friend. Maybe this town won't be so bad after all!

1. What kinds of feelings does this writer show?

2. If this writer were a new student in your class, how do you think he would act on his first day?

EXTRA
Think about a time when you were unhappy and something cheered you up. On a separate piece of paper, write a journal entry about what happened and how you felt.

Does My Writing Sound Like Me? 5

WRITING FOR A SPECIFIC AUDIENCE

NAME _____

SNAKE-Y SURPRISE

Directions: Read each writing example. Answer the questions below the examples on a separate piece of paper.

Example #1:
   A 10-pound snake was found swimming in a pool behind the home of Mr. William Dobbins yesterday afternoon. The snake was discovered in the pool by Mr. Dobbins' son, Robert, when he returned home from school. No one was hurt. The snake was taken to the zoo.

Example #2:
Dear Peggy,
   Hi! I hope you come to visit soon. Guess what? Some people found a super huge snake in their swimming pool. Yuck! Can you believe it? That is really scary. I would probably scream and run three miles up the road until somebody took it away. What's happening with you? Give me a call when you get this letter.
                                                Your friend,
                                                Debbie

1. Which example is written to a friend? How do you know?

2. Which example might be in the newspaper? How do you know?

EXTRA
What if an elephant was found in the pool? How about a lion? Think of an amazing animal you could find in a pool. On a separate piece of paper, write a newspaper article or a letter to a friend to tell about finding it in the pool.

Does My Writing Sound Like Me? 5   **NARRATIVE WRITING**

NAME _____

A DAY IN THE LIFE

Directions: Read the paragraph. Then, answer the questions and follow the directions.

   I wake up in my stall early in the morning. I eat my breakfast oats from the feed bag the woman brings. She brushes my coat and brings me clean water. I trot outside. The sun feels so good and warm. I am so happy that I gallop around the pen. Maybe today the woman will saddle me up and go for a ride in the meadow. I sure hope so.

1. What kind of animal is talking? _____

2. Underline the words that made you think of that animal.

3. How does the animal feel? _____
_____

4. Circle sentences that let you know how the animal feels.

EXTRA

Think about an animal you would like to pretend to be. On a separate piece of paper, write about what you would do and how you might feel. When you are finished, show your writing to a friend and ask her to guess what animal you are pretending to be.

© Carson-Dellosa   32   CD-104036 • Trait-Based Writing Skills 2–3

Does My Writing Sound Like Me? (5)　　　PERSUASIVE WRITING

NAME _____

I THINK I'M RIGHT

Directions: Your teacher has just given you an important issue to think about. Write your opinion about the issue after *I believe*. Then, in just a few words, list at least three reasons for your opinion. Finally, write a paragraph to share with others that tells what you believe and why. Be sure to state your reasons. Use additional paper if needed.

I believe _____

My reasons are:

1. _____

2. _____

3. _____

Additional reasons: _____
_____

My Point of View

_____
_____
_____
_____
_____

Is My Writing Correct?

The young writer has chosen a manageable topic. Specific words and phrases have been selected to paint vivid pictures in readers' minds. The writing flows, allowing the author's voice to shine. What's left to do before this writing masterpiece can be shared with the world? The writer must edit the piece to check for correct spelling, capitalization, punctuation, and grammar.

Create an Editor's Checklist for students to reference. Introduce one skill at a time, adding to the checklist as the year progresses. Students may begin by editing their own writing and then advance to editing their peers' work as skills evolve.

Example of an Editor's Checklist

SYMBOL	EXPLANATION OF THE SYMBOL	EXAMPLE
≡	Capitalize a lowercase letter	marco is my friend.
/	Use a lowercase letter	Tomorrow is my birthday.
⊙	Insert a period	Shelly has two cats⊙
∧	Insert punctuation mark	I feel great! How old are you?
○	Spelling error	Please take my ⟨piktur⟩

Editing for Spelling

Have each student choose a different and interesting paragraph to copy from a social studies or science lesson. When copying the paragraph, ask each student to choose five words to misspell on purpose. Tell them to choose words their classmates should know how to spell. Let students exchange papers. Introduce the editing symbol for marking misspelled words. Have students edit the exchanged papers by finding and marking each misspelled word. Let students return papers and check to see if all misspelled words have been correctly identified.

Is My Writing Correct?

Editing for Capitalization
Review the rules the class has learned regarding capitalization. Introduce the capitalization symbol from the Editor's Checklist. On a piece of chart paper or on a transparency, copy a short, appropriate newspaper article and delete all capitalization. Have students follow along as you read the article aloud. Have students discuss needed changes in capitalization. Choose students to come to the front of the class to make the correct editing marks under each letter to be capitalized and explain why the letter should be capitalized. Then, have students correctly rewrite the article at their desks.

Editing for Punctuation
Review rules students have learned about correct punctuation. Introduce the editing symbols for punctuation. Choose a paragraph to share from a basal reader or trade book that includes the types of punctuation the class has studied. Copy the paragraph, omitting punctuation. Tell students you will read a selection without including any punctuation. Ask students to determine where punctuation is missing and what types are needed. Read the paragraph quickly in a monotone voice without pausing for commas or ending punctuation. Discuss whether the paragraph was easy or difficult to understand without punctuation. Now, read the paragraph more slowly and with correct intonation and pauses to let students hear if a question mark, period, exclamation point, or other type of punctuation should be included. Have students raise their hands each time they hear a need for punctuation. Choose volunteers to identify where punctuation is needed and which type is correct. Finally, distribute copies of the paragraph without punctuation and have students use the editing symbols to insert the punctuation.

Editing for Grammar
Review basic grammar rules students have learned. Ask each student to pick a piece of writing from her writing portfolio. Or, you may choose to exchange copies of student writing with another teacher and remove authors' names in order to prevent identification. Have students edit the writing by underlining any sentences they feel are not grammatically correct. Have them write the corrections above each incorrect sentence. Monitor student activity to ensure students are making appropriate corrections.

Putting an Exclamation Point on It
When students are ready, have them edit their own draft writing for all four conventions—spelling, capitalization, punctuation, and grammar. As skills improve even more, they can also edit their peers' work.

Is My Writing Correct?   6   EDITING FOR SPELLING

NAME _____

CLEVER CAMPERS

Directions: Read the paragraph. Use the Editor's Checklist symbol to mark each misspelled word. Write the correct spelling above the word. Can you find all 10 words?

Example: Please take my *picture* (piktur)

   Camping can be so much fun! Last week my famly went camping in a park near the mowntains. We took lots of stuff becauze we weren't sure what we would need. Dad and I set up the tents while Mom and my brother built a campfire and made lunch. After lunch, we went swimming in the lake while Dad went fishing. He cauht five fish! He clened them and cooked them over the campfire for diner. They tasted great! After diner, we tosted marshmallows and told scary stories. I wasn't really afrad. Later, we crawled inside our tents and tried to sleep. It was quite except for the crickets. The next morning, we got up and started another day of fun. I love camping!

Look at this list of frequently misspelled words. All of the words are spelled correctly. Memorize how to spell each word. Then, spell them to a friend while your friend looks at the paper to check your spelling. Did you spell them correctly?

| chief | choose | cried | don't | except | hero |
| lonely | nickel | paid | said | until | weird |

Is My Writing Correct? 6   EDITING FOR CAPITALIZATION

NAME _____

A GREAT YEAR

Directions: Read the story. Use the Editor's Checklist symbol to show where uppercase letters are needed. You should find 23 errors in all. Then, answer the questions. Use additional paper if needed.

Example: i saw a puppy in the park.

    Last year was lots of fun. in january, we went skiing in Denver, colorado. In february, i got a bunch of candy on valentine's day, and we performed a play at school about the life of martin luther king, jr. My friend, daniel, got to play the part of dr. king. in the spring, my family spent a week at the beach. We saw two baby sharks swimming around the fishing pier! During the summer, I visited my grandparents in texas. I learned all about astronauts at a place named space center houston. Finally, in december, I had the best birthday ever! Mom and dad gave me a puppy. i named him wolf because he looks a little like a baby wolf. Like I said, last year was really lots of fun. I hope next year will be even better!

1. Are there words in the story that sometimes begin with an uppercase letter and sometimes with a lowercase letter? _____

2. If so, what are they, and why are they sometimes capitalized?

_____

3. List 10 words from the story that should always be capitalized.

_____

_____

Is My Writing Correct?   6   EDITING FOR PUNCTUATION

NAME _____

MY LITTLE BROTHER

Directions: Read the paragraph. Use the Editor's Checklist symbol to show where punctuation is needed. Then, write in the correct punctuation. Finally, count how many of each punctuation mark you used and write it below.

Example: Amy, do you like ice cream? I do. It's great!

   My little brother makes me crazy Why did I even have to have a brother He only causes trouble He cries breaks things and runs after the dog Our house was quiet when he wasn't around I guess he is fun sometimes He likes to play hide-and-seek with me He also likes it when I read to him He thinks I'm pretty smart I guess I really do love him but he still makes me crazy

1. periods = _____
2. exclamation points = _____
3. question marks = _____
4. commas = _____

EXTRA

On a separate piece of paper, write a short paragraph about one of your family members. Copy it onto another sheet of paper and leave out all punctuation. Trade papers with a friend. Try to fill in the correct punctuation on your friend's paper. When you are both finished, check each other's work.

TERRIFIC TURKEY

Directions: Read each sentence. Look at the words that are underlined. Circle the best word to use in each sentence. Then, write each sentence correctly.

1. Thanksgiving is **come/coming** soon.

    _____

2. We will **have/had** lots of good food.

    _____

3. Last year, Aunt Pam **brought/brings** green beans.

    _____

4. We all think mashed potatoes **is/are** yummy.

    _____

5. Uncle Bill even **like/likes** the cranberry sauce.

    _____

6. Dad **make/makes** hot biscuits every year.

    _____

7. We all **get/gets** pumpkin pie.

    _____

8. Sometimes I **eat/ate** two pieces!

    _____

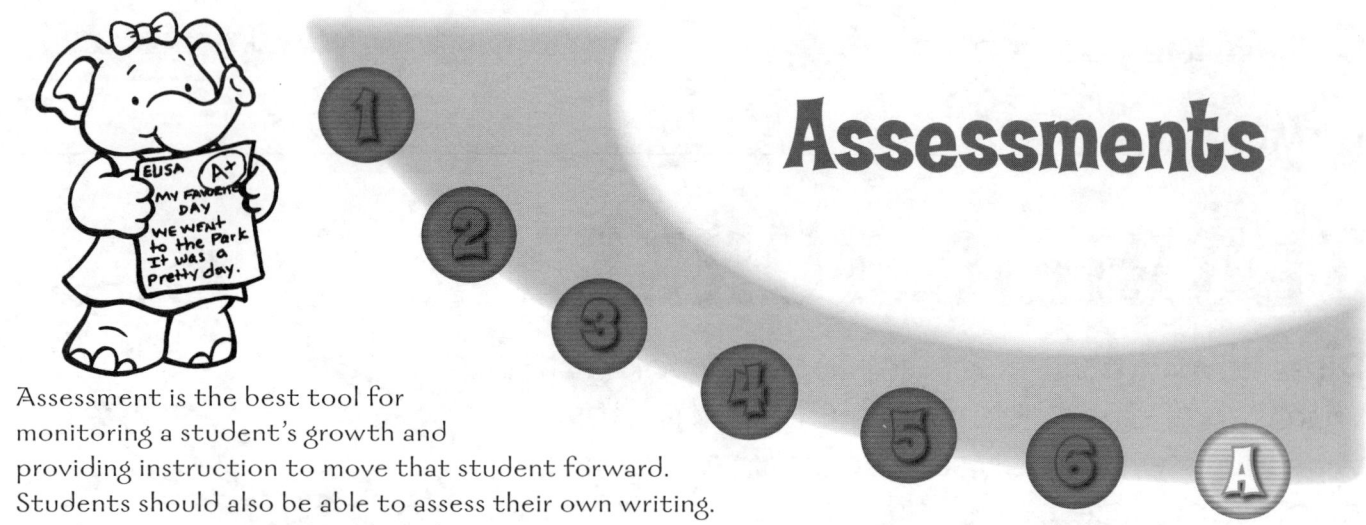

Assessments

Assessment is the best tool for monitoring a student's growth and providing instruction to move that student forward. Students should also be able to assess their own writing. Teacher expectations should not be a secret. As in the proverb, "Give a man a fish and he will eat for a day. Teach a man to fish and he will eat for a lifetime," writing assessment works the same way. Assess a student's piece, and he can correct that assignment. Teach him how to assess his own work, and he will have the tools to improve his writing skills.

Writing Rubric

Writing at higher grade levels becomes more complex. But, for writing at any level to be considered "good," it must have a focused topic, logically presented information, interesting vocabulary, well-constructed sentences, uniqueness, and correct mechanics. A writing rubric scale describes expectations and explains what effective writing looks like. Rubrics are divided into levels that describe the characteristics of writing a student should possess at that point. Students can use guidelines at each level to determine current strengths and identify weaknesses. It is your job to help students understand the rubric's language and to provide opportunities to practice assessing their own and others' writing.

Each student must also understand that her level on the rubric is not a judgment of her worth. It is a gauge of her current writing level that provides a framework for growth. When a student begins a piece, she might look over the rubric to remind herself of good writing characteristics, as well as your expectations for what should be included before an assignment is considered complete. Direct students who ask, "How many sentences/pages should I write?" to check the rubric, paying specific attention to developing areas you have discussed. Using your guidance along with the rubric, students should be able to determine if they have met individualized expectations.

Struggling students may need to have the rubric translated into terms they can understand. You may want to put the information into a writing checklist and reserve the rubric for your teacher assessment. Begin the checklist with just a few items and add to it throughout the year as you introduce new skills.

Example of a Student Writing Checklist for Second and Third Graders

1. My name is on my paper in the correct place.
2. My writing has a title.
3. My topic is not too big.
4. I have shared interesting details about my topic.
5. I have chosen words that paint a picture.
6. My writing sounds like me.
7. I have used uppercase letters in the correct places.
8. I have spelled words correctly.
9. I have used correct punctuation when needed.
10. I am ready to share my writing!

Putting an Exclamation Point on It

Each of the following assessment pages includes an extra challenge activity. Assign these activities to students who need more challenge and are ready to write independently.

Writing Rubric A

Section 1: What Do I Want to Write?

☐ **LEVEL 1**
- No specific topic or main idea
- Details are nonexistent or limited
- Text is too short to develop topic

☐ **LEVEL 2**
- Main idea exists, but is vague
- Details do not relate to the topic
- More information is needed

☐ **LEVEL 3**
- Ideas are clear
- Topic exists, but may be too broad to manage successfully
- Limited details

☐ **LEVEL 4**
- Ideas are clear
- Topic is focused & manageable
- Details relate to topic & provide adequate information

☐ **LEVEL 5**
- Ideas are original & clear
- Topic is focused & manageable
- Supporting details grab readers' interest

Section 2: Does My Writing Have Good Structure?

☐ **LEVEL 1**
- No sense of beginning, middle, & end
- Disorganized
- Lacks direction

☐ **LEVEL 2**
- No clear introduction
- Sequencing, if present, is not logical
- No clear ending

☐ **LEVEL 3**
- Introduction is present, but flat
- Ending exists, but lacks closure
- Organization is loose
- Transitions are attempted

☐ **LEVEL 4**
- Introduction catches readers' interest
- Ending provides adequate closure
- Clear organization
- Transitions may be few, but are logical

☐ **LEVEL 5**
- Fresh "hook" for the introduction
- Ending provides closure, but also leaves readers wishing for more
- Sequence is logical
- Smooth transitions

Section 3: Have I Painted a Clear Picture?

☐ **LEVEL 1**
- Limited vocabulary
- Words used incorrectly
- Lack of communication

☐ **LEVEL 2**
- Simplistic language
- Familiar words used repeatedly
- Dull verbs

☐ **LEVEL 3**
- Correct use of words
- Varied word choices
- Attempts to use colorful language

☐ **LEVEL 4**
- Effective use of language
- Specific word choices enhance interest
- Conveys precise meaning

☐ **LEVEL 5**
- Interesting, rich vocabulary
- Strong verbs
- Descriptive adjectives
- Paints a vivid picture in readers' minds

Writing Rubric A

Section 4: Does My Writing Flow?

☐ **LEVEL 1**
- Sentences begin the same way
- Run-on sentences
- Fragments
- Difficult to read aloud

☐ **LEVEL 2**
- Sentences are correct, but short & choppy
- Lack of variety in sentence structure
- May be read aloud, but doesn't sound natural

☐ **LEVEL 3**
- Sentences generally correct, yet lack interest
- Some variety found in sentence patterns
- Writing sounds routine

☐ **LEVEL 4**
- Generally, sentences are well constructed
- Writing has flow & rhythm
- Easy to read aloud

☐ **LEVEL 5**
- Complete sentences begin in a variety of ways
- Variety of sentence patterns
- Writing has flow & rhythm
- Easy to read aloud

Section 5: Does My Writing Sound Like Me?

☐ **LEVEL 1**
- No sense of audience or purpose
- Does not engage readers
- No sense of commitment to the writing

☐ **LEVEL 2**
- Little sense of audience or purpose
- Occasional attempts to sound sincere by speaking directly to readers
- Writing seems flat

☐ **LEVEL 3**
- Limited sense of audience & purpose
- Writer attempts to convey sincere feelings
- Writing sometimes sounds mechanical

☐ **LEVEL 4**
- Some sense of audience & purpose
- Expresses sincere, honest feelings & engages readers
- Shows some commitment to the writing

☐ **LEVEL 5**
- Writing is appropriate for audience & purpose
- Readers feel a connection to the writer
- Writing sounds natural
- Shows strong commitment to the writing

Section 6: Is My Writing Correct?

☐ **LEVEL 1**
- Misspelled words affect meaning & make writing difficult to read
- Punctuation generally missing or incorrect
- No obvious understanding of paragraphing
- Lack of correct grammar & usage

☐ **LEVEL 2**
- Many spelling errors
- Punctuation often missing or incorrect
- Limited paragraphing
- Frequent grammar & usage errors

☐ **LEVEL 3**
- Correct spelling of many common words
- Punctuation often correct
- Paragraphing usually correct
- Grammar & usage usually correct

☐ **LEVEL 4**
- Few spelling errors
- Punctuation often correct
- Correct paragraphing
- Grammar & usage correct

☐ **LEVEL 5**
- Occasional spelling errors
- No noticeable mistakes in punctuation
- Organized in paragraphs
- Grammar & usage make writing easy to read

Section 1: Assessment — A — WHAT DO I WANT TO WRITE?

NAME _____

TOPIC TRIMMING

Directions: Look at the following topic. Follow the directions to fill in the blanks and find a better topic.

Topic: The Story of Everyone I Know

1. This topic is too big because _____
   _____

2. Three better, more narrow topics are _____
   _____

3. Circle one new topic from your list that you want to write about.

Think about the topic you circled. List three details about the topic that you want to share.

4. _____
5. _____
6. _____

EXTRA

On a separate piece of paper, write a paragraph about your topic. Be sure to include the three details you listed to paint pictures in readers' minds.

CD-104036 • Trait-Based Writing Skills 2–3 — 43 — © Carson-Dellosa

Section 2: Assessment — A — DOES MY WRITING HAVE GOOD STRUCTURE?

NAME _____

A SCARY TALE

Directions: Read the paragraph. Then, follow the directions and answer the questions.

   It all happened so fast. One minute my dad and I were riding in the car, and then it happened. First, the wind started blowing, I mean really blowing, like a giant fan was on the highest setting. Next, the thunder began to boom, and the flashes of sharp, crackly, lightning zapped across the sky every few seconds. Also, the street began to fill with rainwater. It started to wash our car into a ditch! I was really scared, but Dad stayed calm. Our car floated into the ditch and got stuck. We sat there for a while. To me, it seemed like a long time. Finally, the rain stopped. The storm was over. Dad called a tow truck to get us out of the ditch. The car was all muddy, but we were OK. That was one scary car ride!

1. Underline the first two sentences. These sentences are the introduction to the paragraph.

2. Does this introduction make you want to read more? _____

   Why or why not? _____

   _____

3. Circle the words that tell the order in which things happened.

EXTRA

On a separate piece of paper, write a different conclusion to the story. You can make it silly or serious.

Section 3: Assessment Ⓐ HAVE I PAINTED A CLEAR PICTURE?

NAME _____

DESCRIPTIVE DETAILS

Directions: Rewrite the sentences and use a better word for the underlined word in each sentence.

1. The sun in the desert was **hot**.

_____

2. The snowy windowpane felt **cold**.

_____

3. I **went** down the hill.

_____

4. "Run faster!" Suzie **said**.

_____

Write a more descriptive color word for:

red _____   blue _____

yellow _____   green _____

EXTRA

On a separate piece of paper, write about a special day. Tell about how things looked, sounded, smelled, tasted, and felt. Use descriptive words to paint pictures in readers' minds. When you are finished writing, circle your descriptive words.

CD-104036 • Trait-Based Writing Skills 2–3   45   © Carson-Dellosa

Section 4: Assessment Ⓐ   DOES MY WRITING FLOW?

NAME _____

A SHOPPING STORY

Directions: Read the paragraph. Then, follow the directions. You will need a separate piece of paper for 1–3.

    Mom and I went to the grocery store. We chose apples and bananas in the fruit section. We chose lettuce in the vegetable section. We chose corn in the vegetable section. We did not choose carrots. We did not choose potatoes. We chose chicken in the meat section.
Mom said, "Choose some healthy snacks."
"May I have yogurt?" I asked.
"Of course," Mom laughed. "Yogurt is a healthy snack."
"May I have candy, please?" I begged.
"No," Mom sighed, "but you may have popcorn."
That was fine with me because I really like popcorn! We bought our groceries and headed for home to pop a batch.

1. Read the sentences that show the foods chosen in the vegetable section. Combine the two sentences into one sentence.

2. Read the sentences that tell about vegetables that were not chosen. Combine the two sentences into one sentence.

3. Look at the sentences that begin with the words "We chose." Rewrite one sentence to give it a different beginning.

4. Underline the sentences that tell what Mom said.

EXTRA

On a separate piece of paper, write about what foods you would buy if you got to choose. Make your sentences begin differently so that some are long and some are short.

Section 5: Assessment   Ⓐ   **DOES MY WRITING SOUND LIKE ME?**

NAME _____

VOTE "YES!"

Directions: Read the paragraph and answer the questions.

   Hi everyone! We are here to talk about wearing school uniforms. Some people say, "Yeah," and some people say, "Yuck!" I think wearing school uniforms could be a good thing. If we wore uniforms, we wouldn't have to worry about having the right clothes. We wouldn't have to spend lots of money trying to buy the newest stuff every season. Our parents would like that, I'm sure. Also, if we wore uniforms, we could save time every morning because we wouldn't have to figure out what to wear every day. Finally, I think wearing uniforms would be good because you would have to judge people on how they act, not how they look. You would just like people for who they are, not for what they wear. That's the best reason of all. So, I say, "Bring on the uniforms!"

1. Who is the audience? Circle your answer.

   a friend   the school principal   classmates

2. Does the author think students should wear school uniforms? _____

3. List three of the author's reasons: _____

_____

EXTRA

What is your opinion about wearing school uniforms? Write your opinion on a separate piece of paper, telling at least three reasons for your choice.

CD-104036 • Trait-Based Writing Skills 2–3   © Carson-Dellosa

Section 6: Assessment Ⓐ   IS MY WRITING CORRECT?

NAME _____

FANTASTIC FALL

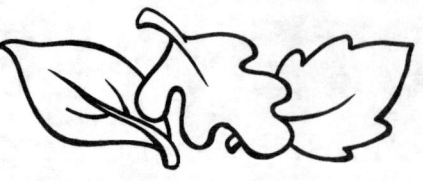

Directions: Read the paragraph. Draw three lines under each lowercase letter that should be an uppercase letter. Put the correct punctuation where it is needed. Circle misspelled words and write the correct spelling above the misspelled word. Use the editors' marks shown below as an example.

≡ capitalize a lowercase letter   ∧ insert punctuation mark

⊙ insert a period   ◯ spelling error

    Fall is my favorate time of year. in september the leaves begin to change colors and it starts to get chilly at night My dog, ranger, likes to jump in the piles of leafes. mom makes hot chocolate to take to the fotball game we like to watch the team from central high school they are the red raiders. go red raiders it is time for the pumpkin harvest in october Do you like pumpkins my little sister thinks they are funny looking. In november we drive into the town of evansville becauze they have a big parade my uncle bob lets my sister sit on his shoulders so that she can see everything. She is so lucky that's OK becauze I always get to have the first piece of pie at diner. i hope you can see why I like fall. what is your favorate season

---

EXTRA

On a separate piece of paper, write about your favorite season and explain why you like it so much.

© Carson-Dellosa   48   CD-104036 • Trait-Based Writing Skills 2–3